Dedicated to my wife Tracey

Thank you for following me on those endless walks around the world!

Check out more photography at:
www.monstermosh37.com
www.monstermosh37.etsy.com

www.ingramcontent.com/pod-product-compliance
Lightning Source LLC
Chambersburg PA
CBHW041511280526
45792CB00004B/1215
9781530962709